A sunflower named

One day Fred planted some sunflower seeds.

2

But only one came up.

"Never mind," said Barney,
"it's a good, strong seedling."

"Yes," said Fred.
"I'm going to call him Bert."

Every day Fred went to see Bert.

Every day he asked Bert how he was.

Hello Bert, how are you?

Sometimes Fred forgot to water Bert.

Sometimes Fred gave Bert
too much water.

But Bert went right on growing . . .

and growing . . .

When Bert's bud opened out into a flower, Fred was very excited.

13

"I'm going to put Bert in the flower show," said Fred.

14

"I know he's the best."

I know he's the best.

15

And Fred was right!

His name
is Bert.

FIRST
PRIZE
FOR
BIGGEST
FLOWER
AWARDED TO:
Fred Pig